HIROSHIMA
AND NAGASAKI

BY ANDREW LANGLEY

T0052494

COMPASS POINT BOOKS
a capstone imprint

Compass Point Books are published by Capstone,
1710 Roe Crest Drive, North Mankato, Minnesota 56003
www.mycapstone.com

Editorial Credits

Sarah Bennett, Jaclyn Jaycox, Angela Kaelberer, Kelli Lageson,
Kathy McColley, and Catherine Neitge.

Photo Credits

Alamy: Everett Collection Historical, 27, World History Archive, 49; DVIC:
NARA, cover; Getty Images: Bettmann, 84, Corbis Historical, 42, 54,
Hulton Archive/FPG, 79, Hulton Archive/Keystone, 6, Keystone/Horace
Abrahams, 57, PhotoQuest, 66, Print Collector/Ann Ronan Pictures, 87,
UIG/Universal History Archive, 9, 11; Library of Congress, 31, 41, 101 (right);
National Archives and Records Administration, 15, 19, 20, 32, 45, 47, 58,
61, 69 (top and bottom), 76, 82, 100 (left and right), 102 (right); Newscom:
Hilary Jane Morgan, 12, Le Pictorium/Active Museum, 22, MCT/U.S. Army
Signal Corps, 62, Photoshot/UPAA, 25, ZUMA Press/Keystone Pictures
USA, 44; Shutterstock: BlueRingMedia, 29, Bule Sky Studio, 91, cowardlion,
21, Dan Thornberg, 68, Everett Historical, 2, 16, 53, 73, 81, 92, 94, 101
(left), 103 (right), Kletr, 34, Milosz Maslanka, 99, Paolo Gianti, 103 (left),
snapgalleria, 24; U.S. Army, 70, 102, (left); Wikimedia: Smyth Report, 37,
United States Department of Energy, 60; XNR Productions, 65

Library of Congress Cataloging-in-Publication Data
Names: Langley, Andrew, 1949– author.
Title: Hiroshima and Nagasaki / by Andrew Langley.
Description: North Mankato, Minnesota : Compass Point Books, a
Capstone imprint, 2018. | Series: Eyewitness to World War II | Includes
bibliographical references and index. | Audience: Age: 10–12. | Audience:
Grade 4 to grade 6.
Identifiers: LCCN 2017010249 | ISBN 9780756555849 (library binding) |
ISBN 9780756555887 (paperback) | ISBN 9780756555924 (ebook pdf)
Subjects: LCSH: Hiroshima-shi (Japan)—History—Bombardment, 1945—
Juvenile literature. | Nagasaki-shi (Japan)—History—Bombardment, 1945—
Juvenile literature. | Atomic bomb—History—20th century—
Juvenile literature.
Classification: LCC D767.25.H6 L329 2018 | DDC 940.54/2521954—dc23
LC record available at https://lccn.loc.gov/2017010249

CONTENTS

The street of "Kawaya Machi." (The famous place of Hiroshima)
通 町 屋 革 (所名島廣)

Hiroshima, Japan, was a bustling city before an atomic bomb left it in ruins on August, 6, 1945.

CHAPTER ONE

FIRE FROM THE SKY

Susumu Kimura was a fifth-grader living with his parents and older sister in Hiroshima, Japan, in 1945. Susumu's country had been at war most of his life, first with China, and since 1941 with the United States and its allies during World War II.

Susumu was used to air attacks by Japan's enemies. When the air raid warning siren sounded at about 7:10 a.m. on August 6, 1945, he and his mother and older sister gathered in a room. His father had already left for work. The family nervously waited about 20 minutes before another siren sounded, signaling that all was clear and people could go about their business.

Susumu's sister, Keiko, who was in seventh grade at First Hiroshima Prefectural Girls' High School, left the house to help tear down damaged buildings in the Dobashi neighborhood in the center of the city. The buildings had been wrecked by air raids. "I'm leaving for work now," Keiko said, picking up her lunch box. Those were the last words Susumu would ever hear his sister say.

After Keiko left, Susumu and his mother planned to go to the train station to buy tickets for a family vacation. Susumu was in the kitchen and his mother was in the next room when a blinding light flashed inside their house. "It flashed from red to yellow just like fireworks," he remembered later. "Everything instantly became pitch dark. You couldn't see an inch ahead."

Susumu found his mother, and they huddled together for several minutes. They had no idea what had just happened. But as their eyes adjusted, they saw that the explosion had leveled the house walls, leaving only the frame standing. As they crawled from the wreckage, an even more horrible sight greeted them. "I saw human bodies in such a state that you couldn't tell whether they were humans or what. . . ," Susumu said later. "There is already a pile of bodies in the road and people are writhing in death agonies."

Amazingly, neither Susumu nor his mother was injured. As they stood in a daze outside their house, Susumu's father rushed up. The explosion had blown him about 15 feet (4.5 meters), but he also was unhurt. The family members knew they had to get somewhere safer. They started walking toward the countryside,

The explosion of the atomic bomb flattened nearly every building in Hiroshima.

leaving a note on the gate for Keiko. That night they slept in the fields. In the morning Susumu's father went into the city to search for Keiko, but fires caused by the explosion prevented him from getting to the Dobashi

VOLUNTEERS BECOME VICTIMS

About 8,000 students from Hiroshima junior and senior high schools were helping tear down damaged buildings at five places in the city—the Prefectural Office, City Hall, Dobashi, Hatchobori, and Tsurumi Bridge—on August 6, 1945. All of the areas were near the Aioi Bridge, which was where the bomb struck.

More than 5,900 of the students were killed. In the Prefectural Office area, 96 percent of 1,891 students were killed. Their bodies were so badly burned that they couldn't be identified. In the Dobashi area, where Keiko Kimura was helping, 1,264 of 1,530 students died. Twelve-year-old Hiroka Nishimoto, a student at Hiroshima Municipal Junior High School, was one of them. His mother searched for days for his body, but found only five buttons from his shirt. Other families found shoes and school bags belonging to their children. Clothing was burned from the bodies of most of the children who weren't killed immediately.

neighborhood. For the next several days the family bicycled into the city to look for Keiko. Later, after their house was rebuilt, they left the gate open every night, but she never returned.

Keiko Kimura was among about 80,000 of Hiroshima's 255,000 inhabitants who were killed or fatally wounded in the first few seconds after an American B-29 bomber dropped a 9,700-pound (4,400-kilogram) atomic bomb on the city. Three days later another U.S. B-29 dropped an atomic bomb on the port city of Nagasaki, about 180 miles (290 kilometers) from Hiroshima. That blast immediately killed or fatally wounded about 45,000 of the city's 240,000 people.

Japanese leaders knew there was no way to keep fighting after the death and devastation caused by the atomic bombs. Japanese Emperor Hirohito announced on August 15 that the country was surrendering to the Allied forces. World War II was over. But for the Japanese people, the horror was just beginning.

Japanese Emperor Hirohito

Archduke Franz Ferdinand and his wife, Sophie, were assassinated while riding in a car on June 28, 1914.

CHAPTER TWO

THE WORLD AT WAR

World War II wasn't the first global conflict. The first began in 1914 when a Serbian, Gavrilo Princip, shot and killed Archduke Franz Ferdinand of Austria-Hungary and his wife. The assassination was the trigger for World War I, which was fought between the Allied forces, including the United States, Great Britain, France, Italy, and Japan, and the Central Powers, including Germany, Austria-Hungary, Turkey, and Bulgaria. At least 8 million soldiers and civilians died during the war. New weapons such as machine guns, explosive shells, poison gas, and airborne bombs caused many of the deaths.

When World War I ended with an Allied victory in November 1918, people throughout the world hoped there would never be another terrible war. But World War I had done nothing to solve international tensions, especially in Europe. Germany received most of the blame for the war and the destruction it brought. Under the Treaty of Versailles, which ended the war, Germany was stripped of its army and much of its territory. It was also ordered to pay reparations to other countries for the damage they had suffered during the war. Germany's economy became increasingly unstable, and during a period of high inflation its currency, the mark, became nearly worthless.

Germans were trying to deal with poverty as well as their feelings of anger and humiliation. In 1933 they elected a new government led by Adolf Hitler and the National Socialist German Workers' (Nazi) Party. Hitler blamed the Treaty of Versailles for ruining Germany's economy and national pride. He also believed that Jewish people in Germany had betrayed their country by pushing government leaders to sign the treaty. Hitler wasn't alone in his feelings. Many people in Germany and other areas of Europe were anti-Semitic, meaning that they hated and resented Jewish people.

Backed by a brutal army and a secret police force, Hitler quickly took complete control of the country. He imprisoned his enemies, crushed his opponents, and promised to make Germany a major world power again by reviving the economy, building a new military, and taking land from other countries. He began by annexing

Adolf Hitler (right) gained popularity after Germany suffered a devastating loss in World War I. He blamed Jewish people for its decline and promised to end Germany's suffering.

Austria and then seizing most of Czechoslovakia. He then set his sights on Poland.

Another nation had also begun building a new empire. Japan had invaded the Manchuria region of northern China in 1931, setting up a puppet government

Japanese invaders marched into Peking in 1937, leading to a war that would kill millions.

with Chinese leaders who were controlled by Japan. By 1937 the Japanese military had seized the Chinese cities of Peking (now Beijing) and Shanghai, starting the Second Sino-Japanese War (1937–1945). Japanese leaders wanted Japan to be the most powerful country in the Pacific region. Japan had few natural resources, such as metal ores and oil, and it was eager to colonize areas that could provide them. The United States, which had been a major trading partner with Japan for raw materials, had stopped much of the trade to punish Japan for its aggressive actions toward China.

The German army invaded Poland on September 1, 1939. Two days later, Great Britain and France declared war on Germany. World War II had begun.

Nations began forming alliances to fight the war. Germany, Italy, and Japan signed the Tripartite Pact on September 27, 1940. They formed the Axis powers, along with Hungary, Romania, Bulgaria, and Slovakia. Germany continued invading other European countries, including Denmark, Norway, Belgium, the Netherlands, and France. Hitler was determined to add Britain to that list, and German planes bombed British cities relentlessly.

The United States managed to stay out of the conflict until December 7, 1941, when Japan staged a surprise attack on Pearl Harbor Naval Base in Hawaii, the home of the U.S. Navy's Pacific Fleet. The bombings killed 2,403 Americans and damaged or destroyed 21 ships and 347 aircraft. The next day the United States declared war on Japan, and four days later it declared war on Germany, joining Great Britain, France, China, and the Soviet Union to form the Allied forces.

Encouraged by the success of the Pearl Harbor attack, Japanese military leaders moved

aggressively into new territory. Japanese forces quickly advanced into Southeast Asia and the Western Pacific. Within four months, Japan had conquered Indonesia,

Smoke poured out of the USS *Arizona* after it was hit during the attack on Pearl Harbor on December 7, 1941.

Malaya, and most of Burma, and it had invaded the Philippines, the Solomon Islands, and New Guinea. Japanese leaders considered invading Australia, bombing the northern area of the country and using midget submarines to attack ships in the harbor of the country's largest city, Sydney, but they decided against it.

The port city of Hiroshima in southwest Japan was the target of several military raids. It was a Japanese army headquarters, a major storage depot, and a place where soldiers were shipped out to other parts of Asia and the Pacific. A Japanese newspaper reporter wrote, "More than a thousand times did the Hiroshima citizens see off with cries of 'Banzai' the troops leaving from the harbor."

U.S. President Franklin D. Roosevelt signed a declaration of war against Japan on December 8, 1941.

The city of Nagasaki, on the southernmost island of Kyushu, was also an important Japanese port and military center. Several weapons factories were there. The two cities' importance to the Japanese military was something U.S. officials would consider later in the war.

HIROSHIMA BEFORE THE BOMBING

Hiroshima had been an important Japanese city for hundreds of years. A feudal lord, Mōri Terumoto, founded the city in 1589 on the delta of the Ota River and the Seto Island Sea. Terumoto built the elegant Hiroshima Castle there as a place from which he could oversee his land.

The city's name means "Broad Island," possibly because the Ota River's channels divide the city into six large islands. During the First Sino-Japanese War in the mid-1890s, the government moved Japan's capital from Tokyo to Hiroshima for safety, and the emperor lived at Hiroshima Castle.

Hiroshima became known as a manufacturing center, especially during the Russo-Japanese War in the early 1900s and during World War I. Factories made weapons and other supplies for the war effort. The weapons and supplies were stored in warehouses and then shipped to battle areas.

Hiroshima Castle stood until the 1945 bombing. It was rebuilt in 1958.

The Hiroshima Castle as it stands today

Democritus was the first to develop the concept of an atom, laying the foundation for future scientists to build on the idea.

CHAPTER THREE

DEVELOPING THE A-BOMB

War and conflict have been a part of life since the beginning of history. New weapons to help people wage war against each other continue to be developed and improved. By the late 1930s, building the most deadly and powerful weapon ever made—the atomic bomb—became possible because of scientific discoveries. The race to build an atomic bomb and gain an unbeatable advantage in the coming world war began.

The effort to develop atomic power began with the ancient Greeks. More than 2,400 years ago, Greek philosopher Democritus wrote that all matter was made of many tiny particles. He called these particles atoms, which meant "things which cannot be split." No one could prove his theory, however.

Hundreds of years later, other scientists added to the Democritus theory. In the 1750s Croatian scientist Rudjer Boscovich said that atoms were not really the smallest units in the universe because they contained even tinier particles. British physicist Joseph John Thomson in 1897 discovered one of the particles, which he called the electron. Another physicist, New Zealander Ernest Rutherford, discovered the nucleus—the particle at the center of the atom—in 1911. A former student of Rutherford, James Chadwick, discovered in 1932 that atoms also contain particles called neutrons.

The atom is made up of protons, neutrons, and electrons.

Ernest Rutherford became known as the father of nuclear physics.

By that time it was known that atoms had neutrons and protons in their nuclei, with electrons moving around outside the nuclei. Protons are positively charged, electrons are negatively charged, and neutrons have no charge. Electrons whiz around the empty space outside the nucleus. An atom of the element hydrogen contains one proton and one electron, but no neutrons. An atom of uranium contains 92 protons, 146 neutrons, and 92 electrons.

Scientists wanted to learn more about the composition of atoms. They knew that to do that, they needed to break one apart. But how would you split such a tiny object?

The answer was to use other atoms. Some substances have atoms that are naturally unstable. This means they are always changing and emitting a stream of particles, including electrons and parts of the nucleus. This process is called radioactivity. Scientists discovered that they could use these flying radioactive particles to split atoms. The early atomic physicists didn't realize that their discoveries would have any practical use. They were only trying to understand how the building blocks of matter were put together.

The answers to the scientists' questions came mainly from work in German laboratories. German chemist Otto Hahn began working with Austrian physicist Lise Meitner in 1907 in Berlin. They were later joined by chemist Friedrich Strassmann. Much of their work involved experiments with a radioactive element, uranium. In 1938 they discovered that when they used neutrons to bombard an atom of uranium, the atom split into two different elements, barium and krypton.

A year later, Meitner and her nephew, physicist Otto Frisch, took the results one step further. They showed

Lise Meitner and Otto Hahn worked together for 30 years. They were nominated for the Nobel Prize for 10 consecutive years for their discoveries.

that the atoms in the uranium had been split. They called this process "nuclear fission." The process of fission produced more energy than it had used. The incredible power inside the atom had been unlocked.

Scientists realized that they had discovered a source of power with unknown potential. When the neutrons split an atom, it released energy as well as more neutrons. The neutrons shot off to split neighboring atoms, which themselves gave off more neutrons. The fission and the release of energy would continue as long as there were atoms to split. Scientists theorized that the result of such a chain reaction would be a huge explosion. But how huge? And how would it be controlled? No one knew, but scientists and government leaders alike were eager to learn. They all knew that the country that built the first atomic weapon would control the fate of the world.

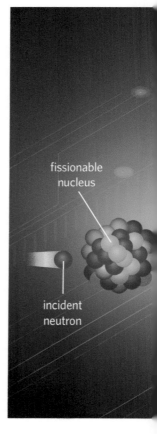

fissionable nucleus

incident neutron

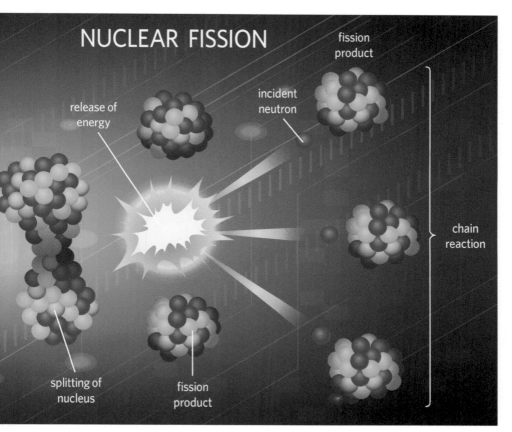

NUCLEAR FISSION

fission product

incident neutron

release of energy

chain reaction

splitting of nucleus

fission product

Before the discovery of nuclear fission, it was thought impossible that a uranium nucleus could be split in two. This discovery led to the making of the first atomic bomb.

A NUCLEAR PIONEER

Lise Meitner was a scientist at a time when scientific study wasn't open to many women. She was born in 1878 in Vienna, Austria, the third of eight children in a Jewish family. She showed early promise in math, but she was only allowed to attend school until age 14. At the time few colleges admitted women, especially to study subjects such as science and math. But when Meitner was 21, the University of Vienna decided to admit women. Meitner studied for nearly two years to earn her high school diploma. She then took and passed the university admittance exam. She earned a doctorate in physics in 1906, and the next year she went to Berlin, Germany, to study with the famed physicist Max Planck.

In Berlin Meitner teamed with chemist Otto Hahn and worked with him for 30 years. They discovered the element protactinium in 1918. Twenty years later, they and Friedrich Strassmann did their ground-breaking experiments with uranium. But their collaboration ended later that year when Germany annexed Austria. Even though Meitner had earlier converted to Christianity, she was still a Jew in the eyes of the

and weapons. But when the Royal Swedish Academy of Sciences awarded the 1944 Nobel Prize in Chemistry for the discovery of nuclear fission, Otto Hahn alone received the prize. He refused to give Meitner any credit for her role.

Meitner continued her work until she retired in 1960. For what she and her colleagues had accomplished, the United States gave Meitner, Hahn, and Strassmann the Enrico Fermi Presidential Award in 1966, two years before Meitner died.

Nazis and therefore a target for persecution. She fled to Sweden, where she and her nephew, physicist Otto Frisch, developed the concept of nuclear fission.

Meitner's discoveries contributed greatly to the development of nuclear energy

Jewish people living in Germany were sent to concentration camps during the Holocaust. Those that weren't immediately murdered were forced to work 14 to 16 hours a day with no food or water. Many of them died of starvation.

CHAPTER FOUR

THE BOMB RACE

After the discovery of nuclear fission, Germany seemed very likely to be the first country to develop a nuclear weapon. The country had a large supply of uranium, the raw material for a chain reaction. And several of the world's greatest physicists lived in Germany or Austria, including those who did the pioneering work on nuclear fission.

But Hitler's crusade against Jewish people worked against him. As Germany passed more laws discriminating against Jewish people and as acts of violence against them increased, many of them decided to leave. By October 1941 about 360,000 Jews—nearly 70 percent of the country's total Jewish population—had immigrated to other European

A RADIOACTIVE METAL

Uranium occurs naturally in Earth's crust, as well as in ocean water. German chemist Martin Klaproth discovered the element in 1789 and named it after the planet Uranus.

Like all elements, uranium is found in various forms called isotopes. The isotopes differ because of the number of neutrons in their nuclei. Three uranium isotopes are found in Earth's crust: uranium-238, uranium-234, and uranium-235. Uranium-238 is the most common, composing 99.3 percent of Earth's uranium. There is only a trace amount of uranium-234. Uranium-235 is much more likely to produce fission than uranium-238, but it makes up just 0.7 percent of Earth's supply. That made obtaining enough uranium to build nuclear bombs a challenge for the scientists working on the atomic bomb. They solved this problem by enriching uranium samples to increase their proportion of U-235. The scientists tested four processes to enrich the uranium—electromagnetic separation, gaseous diffusion, liquid thermal diffusion, and centrifugation. They found that gaseous diffusion worked best and built a plant in Oak Ridge, Tennessee, for the process.

countries, the United States, Palestine, or Central and South America. They included top scientists such as Hans Bethe, Lise Meitner, Leo Szilard, and Edward Teller. Leaving was a wise decision. The Nazis decided to exterminate the Jewish people who remained in Germany and its occupied countries. About 6 million Jews died during the Holocaust.

The most famous Jewish scientist was physicist Albert Einstein, who had developed the special theory of relativity in 1905. This theory, Energy = Matter x Speed of Light^2 in equation form, helped scientists determine how much energy could potentially be released in a chain reaction. When the Nazis came to power in 1933, Einstein left Germany and moved to the United States to work at the Institute for Advanced Study in Princeton, New Jersey.

Einstein spent the summer of 1939 on Long Island, New York. One day in July he was visited by scientists Leo Szilard and Edward Teller. They were concerned that Germany, with its large supply of uranium, could be the first country to develop a nuclear weapon.

They asked Einstein to send a letter to President Franklin D. Roosevelt warning him of what could happen to the world if Germany developed an atomic bomb. Szilard planned to ask Alexander Sachs, an economist who was a close friend of Roosevelt's, to give Einstein's letter to the president.

Einstein agreed to write the letter. Dated August 2, 1939, it read, in part: "In the course of the last four months it has been made probable—through the work of Joliot in France as well as Fermi and Szilard in America—that it may become possible to set up a nuclear chain reaction in a large mass of uranium, by which vast amounts of power and large quantities of new radium-like elements would be generated. Now it appears almost certain that this could be achieved in the immediate future.

"This new phenomenon would also lead to the construction of bombs, and it is conceivable—though much less certain—that extremely powerful bombs of a new type may thus be constructed. A single bomb of this type, carried by boat and exploded in a port, might very

Albert Einstein
Old Grove Rd.
Nassau Point
Peconic, Long Island

August 2nd, 1939

F.D. Roosevelt,
President of the United States,
White House
Washington, D.C.

Sir:

    Some recent work by E.Fermi and L. Szilard, which has been com-
municated to me in manuscript, leads me to expect that the element uranium may be turned into a new and important source of energy in the immediate future. Certain aspects of the situation which has arisen seem
to call for watchfulness and, if necessary, quick action on the part
of the Administration. I believe therefore that it is my duty to bring
to your attention the following facts and recommendations:

    In the course of the last four months it has been made probable -
through the work of Joliot in France as well as Fermi and Szilard in
America - that it may become possible to set up a nuclear chain reaction
in a large mass of uranium,by which vast amounts of power and large quantities of new radium-like elements would be generated. Now it appears
almost certain that this could be achieved in the immediate future.

    This new phenomenon would also lead to the construction of bombs,
and it is conceivable - though much less certain - that extremely powerful bombs of a new type may thus be constructed. A single bomb of this
type, carried by boat and exploded in a port, might very well destroy
the whole port together with some of the surrounding territory. However,
such bombs might very well prove to be too heavy for transportation by
air.

ium in moderate ...
rmer Czechoslovakia,
ongo.

ble to have some
and the group
e possible way
task a person
n inofficial

nformed of the
Government action,
giving particular attention to the problem of securing a supply of uranium ore for the United States;

    b) to speed up the experimental work,which is at present being car-
ried on within the limits of the budgets of University laboratories, by
providing funds, if such funds be required, through his contacts with
private persons who are willing to make contributions for this cause,
and perhaps also by obtaining the co-operation of industrial laboratories
which have the necessary equipment.

    I understand that Germany has actually stopped the sale of uranium
from the Czechoslovakian mines which she has taken over. That she should
have taken such early action might perhaps be understood on the ground
that the son of the German Under-Secretary of State, von Weizsäcker, is
attached to the Kaiser-Wilhelm-Institut in Berlin where some of the
American work on uranium is now being repeated.

Yours very truly,
A. Einstein
(Albert Einstein)

The letter sent to President Franklin D. Roosevelt from Albert Einstein encouraged the United States to speed up research on atomic energy.

well destroy the whole port together with some of the surrounding territory."

Einstein advised Roosevelt to investigate potential U.S. sources of uranium and to give more money to U.S. laboratories to allow them to increase their research. Szilard sent the letter to Sachs about two weeks later. But Sachs took his time delivering the letter to Roosevelt. He finally met with the president on October 11. But instead of simply handing Roosevelt the letter, Sachs had prepared an 800-word summary of the letter, which he read to the president.

After listening to Sachs, Roosevelt said, "Alex, what you are after is to see that the Nazis don't blow us up."

"Precisely," Sachs replied.

Roosevelt yelled for his military adviser and aide, General Edwin Watson. "Pa!" Roosevelt said, using Watson's nickname. "This requires action!"

Roosevelt, Sachs, and the scientists didn't know that although German scientists were eager to develop an atomic weapon, Hitler didn't believe it was a good idea. He thought Germany could improve conventional weapons that could be used earlier in the war. He refused to provide a lot of money for nuclear weapons research. The Nazi government never developed an atomic bomb.

A GENIUS MIND

Albert Einstein is considered by many to have had the greatest scientific mind in history. He was born to Jewish parents in Ulm, Germany, in 1879. He was an intelligent child and particularly good at math, but he disliked the way the subjects were taught and earned only average grades. But he read as much as he could about science and math during his free time.

Einstein's family moved to Italy when he was 15, and he followed shortly afterward. He finished high school in 1896 in Switzerland and then attended the Federal Polytechnic School in Zurich.

After graduating in 1900, he became a Swiss citizen. Einstein searched unsuccessfully for a job until 1902, when he was hired as an examiner by the Swiss Patent Office in Bern. He spent the next nine years working in the patent office during the day and devoting his evenings to scientific research and experiments. In 1905 he published five scientific papers, including one on his special theory of relativity.

After leaving the patent office, Einstein taught theoretical physics at universities in Germany and Switzerland. In 1915 he was teaching at the University of Berlin when he published his general theory of relativity. He was awarded the Nobel Prize for Physics in 1921.

As the Nazi Party took power in Germany, Einstein decided to immigrate to the United States. He moved in 1933 to Princeton, New Jersey, where he worked at the Institute for Advanced Study. He became a dual American and Swiss citizen in 1940. Because of his socialist political views, the U.S. Army didn't allow him to work on the scientific team that built the atomic bomb. He continued his work in the United States until his death in 1955.

Einstein was upset by the bombings of Hiroshima and Nagasaki and regretted that

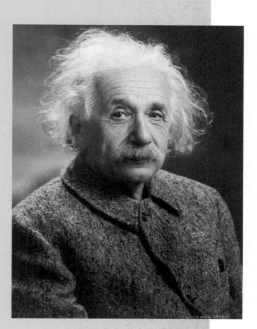

he played even a small role in developing the nuclear bomb. In an interview with Newsweek magazine, he said, "Had I known that the Germans would not succeed in developing an atomic bomb, I would have done nothing."

Enrico Fermi (front row, left) led the effort at the University of Chicago to create the world's first nuclear reactor.

CHAPTER FIVE

THE MANHATTAN PROJECT

President Roosevelt was quick to act on Albert Einstein's warning letter. He appointed physicist Lyman Briggs, who was the head of the National Bureau of Standards, to lead a new Advisory Committee on Uranium. Briggs asked Army Lieutenant Colonel Keith Adamson and Navy Commander Gilbert Hoover to join him.

The committee first met on October 21, 1939. Physicists Leo Szilard, Edward Teller, and Eugene Wigner also attended, along with Fred Mohler of the National Bureau of Standards and Richard Roberts of the Carnegie Institution of Washington, a research organization. Einstein was invited but didn't attend. In early 1940 the uranium committee recommended that the

U.S. government pay for research on atomic energy. The government authorized $6,000—about $100,000 in today's dollars.

The uranium committee was absorbed into a new government committee, the National Defense Research Committee (NDRC), in June 1940. Vannevar Bush, an engineer and inventor, led this committee. A year later President Roosevelt signed an executive order creating a new government agency, the Office of Scientific Research and Development. Bush became its director, reporting directly to Roosevelt. The NDRC was now part of this agency. Bush teamed up with the new NDRC director, James Conant, to speed up research and development on atomic energy. They added famed Italian physicist Enrico Fermi and American chemist Harold Urey to the uranium committee.

Enrico Fermi built the world's first nuclear reactor.

The attack on Pearl Harbor on December 7, 1941, was one of the deadliest days in U.S. Navy history. A total of 2,403 Americans died that day.

Bush met with President Roosevelt and Vice President Henry A. Wallace on October 9, 1941. Roosevelt told Bush to determine what materials would be needed and how much it would cost to build an atomic weapon. Bush sent a report to Roosevelt on November 27. Just 10 days later, Japan attacked Pearl Harbor. With the United

States now fighting World War II, the atomic bomb went from a possible weapon to one the U.S. government knew it needed to have before the enemy did.

The attack on Pearl Harbor was a huge blow to the U.S. military. But there was one bright spot. None of the U.S. aircraft carriers were at Pearl Harbor on December 7. So the big ships were able to go into combat immediately, and they played a very important part in the Allied fight. U.S. bombers made their first raid on Tokyo in April 1942. The raid did little damage, but it showed Japanese leaders that their country was vulnerable to attack. Then the U.S. Navy stopped the Japanese advance in the Pacific with important victories at the Battle of the Coral Sea and the Battle of Midway.

Intelligence reports from overseas increased the Allies' worries about an enemy bomb. James Conant gave an

alarming report in May 1942 on German progress based
on information he had received from secret agents:
"If they are hard at work, they cannot be far behind us.

The Battle of Midway is considered one of the most decisive battles of World War II. The U.S.
succeeded in destroying four Japanese aircraft carriers during the four-day sea-and-air battle.

There are still plenty of competent scientists left in Germany. They may be ahead of us by as much as a year."

Japanese naval leaders thought the only practical use of nuclear energy would be to power its ships. But physicist Tokutaro Hagiwara was working hard on nuclear research at the University of Kyoto. The Allies couldn't afford to waste any time.

Research on the bomb was taking place in several laboratories across the United States—the University of California at Berkeley, Columbia University in New York City, and the University of Chicago in Illinois. All were making progress, especially the scientists at Berkeley, who could enrich uranium using isotope separation. When Bush told Roosevelt a U.S. atomic bomb could be ready by 1944, Roosevelt said, "I think the whole thing should be pushed not only in regard to development, but also with due regard to time. This is very much of the essence."

The bomb project, still top secret, was officially headquartered in New York City in the Manhattan

Engineer District, a division of the U.S. Army Corps of Engineers. The district's normal-sounding name was used to keep the bomb-development program, later called the Manhattan Project, a secret.

The army assigned Colonel Leslie R. Groves to lead the Manhattan Project on September 17, 1942, and six days later promoted him to brigadier general. Groves was a career army officer who had helped oversee the building of the Pentagon in Washington, D.C., as the headquarters of the War Department.

Groves didn't have a science background, so he insisted that a scientist should direct the project. He chose a physicist and professor at the University of California at Berkeley, J. Robert Oppenheimer. Groves' next job was to find a large supply of uranium. A warehouse on Staten

Leslie Groves (left) and Robert Oppenheimer were both instrumental to the success of the Manhattan Project.

LESLIE GROVES

Leslie Groves was born in New York in 1896. He graduated fourth in his class at the U.S. Military Academy at West Point, New York, in 1918 and served briefly in World War I. Groves spent the years between the wars working for the Office of the Chief of Engineers in Washington, D.C. When the United States entered World War II, Groves wanted to be on active duty overseas. He was disappointed with his assignment leading the Manhattan Project. But he quickly changed his mind when his commanding officer, Lieutenant General Brehon Somervell, assured him that in his new role he could help the Allies win the war.

Groves was single-minded, blunt, and determined to make the project a success. His district engineer on the Manhattan Project was Colonel Kenneth Nichols. He later said of his boss, "He is always a driver, never a praiser. He is abrasive and sarcastic . . . He is the most egotistical man I know. He knows he is right and so sticks by his decision. He abounds with energy and expects everyone to work as hard, or even harder, than he does . . . if I had to do my part of the atomic bomb project over again and had the privilege of picking my boss, I would pick General Groves."

Groves retired from the army in 1948. He then became vice president of the pioneering computer company Sperry Rand Corporation. He died in 1970.

Island, New York, contained 1,200 tons of high-grade uranium ore. Groves sent someone to buy the uranium and move it to Chicago. Enrico Fermi used it to build the world's first nuclear reactor in a little-used squash court at the University of Chicago. If Fermi's experiment succeeded, it would prove that a chain reaction could produce enough energy for a vast explosion. Just as important, the experiment would show that the chain reaction could be controlled.

When Fermi successfully tested the reactor on December 2, 1942, it proved the theory of nuclear fission. Until then, scientists hadn't been sure that the process was possible. It was a cause for celebration for most of the scientists working on the Manhattan Project. But others worried that a weapon capable of instantly killing thousands of people was now a reality. Leo Szilard was one of them. He said later, "I shook hands with Fermi, and I said that I thought this day would go down as a black day in the history of mankind."

FERMI'S NUCLEAR REACTOR

To build the nuclear reactor, workers began by stacking graphite blocks in a circular pile. The blocks contained small spheres of radioactive uranium. The graphite slowed the radioactivity of the uranium. Even so, as the pile grew higher, the energy produced by the escaping radioactive particles increased. The scientists pushed special "control rods" into the pile to stop the radioactivity.

The stacked blocks reached 57 layers on December 2, 1942. Then the team began to pull out the control rods one by one. Slowly the pile came to life as the neutrons became active. Machines recorded each escaping neutron, clicking every time one was counted.

The clicks came faster until they merged into a single roar of noise. Fermi raised his hand and said, "The pile has gone critical." He meant that the experiment was a success. Fermi had created a self-sustaining atomic chain reaction. He also proved that humans could control and use atomic power.

The Chicago Pile-1, the world's first nuclear reactor, was built under the football field at the University of Chicago.

The Los Alamos National Laboratory was a secret lab where some of the world's leading scientists built the atomic bombs that killed thousands and ended World War II.

CHAPTER SIX

TESTING THE BOMB

Leslie Groves and Robert Oppenheimer knew that something that needed to be kept secret and was as dangerous as an atomic bomb couldn't be built in a large city such as Chicago. They decided to move the Manhattan Project to a remote site in the New Mexico desert. A laboratory was built at the former site of the Los Alamos Boys Ranch School, near Santa Fe. By summer 1943, an entire community had sprung up around the secret lab.

Oppenheimer's team included some of the world's best chemists, physicists, and engineers. During 1943 and 1944, they worked on the complicated task of designing and manufacturing the bomb.

Meanwhile, the Allies were winning the war in Europe. Allied troops landed in Italy in July 1943 and in France in June 1944. Troops moved into Germany in September 1944 and began forcing German soldiers to retreat from the invaded countries. In January 1945 the Allies defeated the German army at the Battle of the Bulge in Belgium, France, and Luxembourg.

The Allies surrounded the German capital of Berlin in April 1945. Hitler and his top aides retreated to an underground bunker in the city. Hitler committed suicide there on April 30, and Germany surrendered May 8. The war in Europe was over. But President Roosevelt didn't live to see it. He died of a stroke on April 12. His vice president, Harry S. Truman, became president.

Germany's surrender left only Japan to fight for the Axis powers. American and Australian forces had driven the Japanese from the jungles of New Guinea and the Solomon Islands and then from the islands of the central Pacific. But the battles were long and caused many casualties. The Allies attacked the Japanese-controlled

U.S. soldiers waved American flags after capturing the city of Nuremberg, Germany.

Philippine Islands in October 1944. During the six-month battle, about 350,000 Japanese soldiers died, while the Americans lost about 14,000.

By early 1945 the Allies had retaken all the territory that the Japanese had invaded, and they had taken control of the skies and the sea. U.S. B-29 bombers destroyed Japan's factories and ports, while submarines sank ships that brought food and other essential supplies to the Japanese. In March a massive bombing raid on

During World War II, the U.S. military bombed 67 cities in Japan.

the capital, Tokyo, killed about 100,000 people and left another million homeless.

Still the Japanese refused to surrender. In the Japanese culture, surrendering was considered far worse than being killed in battle. Soldiers and leaders believed that surrendering would bring dishonor to their families and to Japan itself. In the past, Japanese warriors had killed themselves with their own swords rather than be captured. The Japanese soldiers of World War II were prepared to fight to the death.

Allied leaders began to plan for a final invasion of the Japanese mainland, which would take place in November 1945. They knew the invasion would likely kill millions of Japanese soldiers and civilians, as well as about a million Allied soldiers.

President Harry Truman hadn't known of the Manhattan Project until Roosevelt died. At that point, he and the other Allied leaders had a major decision to make. The Allies hoped that just the threat of the atomic bomb would be enough to make Japan surrender, thus saving countless military and civilian lives. But first the leaders had to be sure the bomb would work as expected. They would have to detonate a test bomb.

By July 1945 the Manhattan Project team was ready to perform its final test on the first bomb, which Oppenheimer called Trinity. The test site was 210 miles (338 km) south of Los Alamos in a remote area of the Alamogordo Bombing Range. Crew members had built a 100-foot (30-meter) steel tower at the site. On July 15 they assembled the bomb and carefully hoisted it to the top of the tower. Then they waited. The test was scheduled for 4:00 in the morning of July 16, but heavy rain pushed back the test time. The skies cleared about 4:00 and the test was rescheduled for 5:30. Some team members took cover in nearby bunkers, while others went as far as 20 miles (32 km) away to watch.

At 5:30 the bomb was detonated. The scientists saw something no human had ever seen before. "Suddenly there was an enormous flash of light," physicist Isidor

A crew assembled Trinity at the base of the tower on the morning of July 16, 1945.

Rabi wrote later. "It blasted; it pounced; it bored its way right through you. It looked menacing. A new thing had been born."

The fireball reminded Robert Oppenheimer of a line from ancient Hindu scripture: "Now I am become death, the destroyer of worlds."

The test bomb proved that a nuclear explosion caused an almost unbelievable amount of destruction. The blast turned the asphalt around

A huge mushroom cloud rose from the ground where the bomb was detonated in New Mexico.

the tower to sand and knocked some of the watching team members to the ground. Some were temporarily blinded. Most of the steel tower was vaporized, simply disappearing into thin air. At the base camp, Bush shook hands with Conant and Groves. Their work was done. Now it was up to the world's leaders to decide what to do with it.

Allied leaders met at the Potsdam Conference to discuss the terms of Japan's surrender. Seated in the front row are British Prime Minister Clement Attlee (from left), U.S. President Harry S. Truman, and Soviet leader Josef Stalin.

CHAPTER SEVEN

A FATEFUL MISSION

On the day of the test at Los Alamos, the leaders of the three main Allied nations—the United States, Great Britain, and the Soviet Union—were traveling to Potsdam, Germany. The Potsdam Conference took place from July 17 to August 2, 1945. The United States, Britain, and China on July 26 issued what was called the Potsdam Declaration, which stated the Allies' terms for Japan's surrender. The Soviet Union wasn't at war with Japan, so it didn't participate in the proclamation. The declaration didn't mention the atomic bomb, but it promised "prompt and utter destruction" if Japan didn't surrender.

The Japanese leaders rejected the surrender terms and went on fighting. They had no way of knowing that the parts for two atomic bombs were already being shipped to Tinian, an island in the Marianas Islands near Japan. Tinian was a base for the B-29 bombers of the U.S. Air Force. Army Air Corps Colonel Paul Tibbets and the crew of the 509th Composite Group, which was formed for the atomic bomb mission, had been training at Tinian since March 1945.

Several Japanese cities had been considered possible targets for the atomic bombs, including Kyoto, Yokohama, Niigata, Kokura, Hiroshima, and Nagasaki. One reason Hiroshima was selected was that it didn't have an Allied prisoner-of-war camp nearby, so no Allied troops would die in the blast. Nagasaki was the home of the Mitsubishi factory, which had made the torpedoes used in the devastating attack at Pearl Harbor.

The first bomb, nicknamed "Little Boy," was ready by July 31. Plans were made to drop the bomb on Hiroshima the next day, but a storm delayed the mission. Meanwhile, the second bomb, nicknamed "Fat Man," was being assembled.

Tibbets called his crew members together on August 3. Until that moment, they hadn't been told

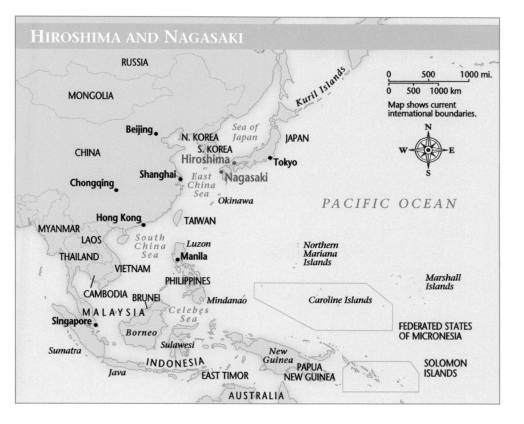

HIROSHIMA AND NAGASAKI

exactly why they were there. They learned that they were going to drop the most destructive weapon ever made, probably on August 6. Stunned, the men weren't sure how to react. Sergeant Abe Spitzer, a radio operator, wrote in his diary, "It is like some weird dream conceived by one with too vivid an imagination."

ENOLA GAY

Thomas Ferebee, Paul Tibbets, Theodore Van Kirk, and Robert Lewis were part of the crew that dropped the first atomic bomb on Hiroshima.

Crewman	Position
Colonel Paul Tibbets	Commander
Captain Robert Lewis	Copilot
Captain Theodore Van Kirk	Navigator
Major Thomas Ferebee	Bombardier
Lieutenant Jacob Beser	Electronic Countermeasures
Sergeant Joseph Stiborik	Radar Operator
Private Richard Nelson	Radar Operator
Staff Sergeant Wyatt Duzenbury	Flight Engineer
Staff Sergeant George Robert "Bob" Caron	Tail Gunner
Captain William "Deke" Parsons	Weaponeer
2nd Lieutenant Morris "Dick" Jeppson	Ordnance Expert
Sergeant Robert Shumard	Assistant Flight Engineer

At 2 p.m. on August 5 the waiting crew members received a report forecasting good weather for the next day for Hiroshima. General Curtis LeMay, commander of the Army Air Corps, confirmed that the mission would be the next day. Tibbets had the B-29 he would fly—the one that would drop Little Boy—painted with his mother's first and middle name, Enola Gay.

Tibbets and his crew got very little sleep that night. Their final briefing was scheduled for midnight. After the briefing the crew ate breakfast and posed for photos with the *Enola Gay*. Takeoff was scheduled for 2:45 a.m.

Dressed in flak suits and dark goggles, Tibbets and the 11 crew members boarded the *Enola Gay*. It was a difficult takeoff, because the B-29 was carrying 7,000 pounds (3,175 kg) of fuel in addition to the 9,700-pound (4,400-kg) bomb. The aircraft weighed more than 65 tons in all. The *Enola Gay* was almost at the end of the runway when it lumbered into the air and set off for Hiroshima.

At 3 a.m. Captain Deke Parsons and 2nd Lieutenant Dick Jeppson climbed into the bomb bay to finish final assembly of Little Boy. Shortly before 6 a.m., the *Enola Gay* flew over Iwo Jima island, where it met its two escort planes. They were about two hours away from their target.

At 7:30 Parsons climbed into the bomb bay to arm Little Boy. It was the last step of the mission before releasing the bomb.

Enola Gay carried 12 crew members and Little Boy to Hiroshima on August 6, 1945.

At 8:50 a.m.—7:50 Hiroshima time—the *Enola Gay* began its final approach to the target area. The bombardier, Major Thomas Ferebee, took control of the plane from Tibbets. He spotted the T-shaped Aioi Bridge at the center of the city. That was the target. At 8:15 a.m. Hiroshima time, Ferebee released Little Boy. It was set to explode in 43 seconds.

Little Boy detonated about 2,000 feet (610 meters) above the city. Within a split second, it produced a gigantic fireball so hot that the temperature directly under it reached 5,400 degrees Fahrenheit (2,982 degrees Celsius). The blast of intense heat instantly killed almost all people within half a mile. Their skin was scorched to carbon, and their internal organs boiled away.

FAT MAN AND LITTLE BOY

American physicist and Manhattan Project team member Robert Serber was the person who invented the code names for the atomic bombs, based on their shapes. Fat Man was large and round, while Little Boy was smaller. A third design, Thin Man, was never produced.

Little Boy and Fat Man were not the same kind of atomic bomb, and they worked differently. Little Boy contained uranium. It was detonated by firing one piece of uranium into another, which started a chain reaction. The second bomb contained plutonium, which is even more radioactive than uranium. It was surrounded by explosives. When they exploded, they squashed the plutonium from all sides, causing an immediate chain reaction.

Little Boy	
Length: 10 feet (3 m)	
Diameter: 28 inches (71 cm)	
Weight: 9,700 pounds (4,400 kg)	

Fat Man	
Length: 10 feet 8 inches (3.25 m)	
Diameter: 60.25 inches (153 cm)	
Weight: 10,265 pounds (4,656 kg)	

Birds turned to ash in midair. Even people 2 miles (3 km) from the center of the blast suffered severe burns.

The blinding light acted like a giant camera. Three thousand times as powerful as sunlight, it bleached the surfaces of the city. The shadows of people, carts, ladders, telegraph poles, and leaves created dark patches that stood out against the whitened materials beneath them. Dark clothing burned more easily than light-colored clothes, leaving bizarre patterns on the skin. Anyone

The view from *Enola Gay* moments after dropping the atomic bomb on Hiroshima.

who looked directly at the flash suffered permanent eye damage.

A few moments after the light and heat came the explosion's shock waves. From the center of the blast, the waves shot outward at 2 miles (3 km) per second like an extremely powerful wind.

High above, the *Enola Gay* crew watched the horror unfolding. They saw an enormous fireball and felt the shock waves, which made the aircraft bounce in midair. Then out of the blast a mushroom cloud boiled up into the sky above Hiroshima. Captain Robert Lewis, the copilot, said he could somehow taste the atomic explosion. It tasted like lead. Lewis wrote in his flight journal: "If I live a hundred years, I'll never quite get these few minutes out of my mind."

A few minutes before the bomb dropped, Hiroshima had been a city of buildings and streets. Now Lewis could barely make out anything except smoke and fire and the enormous mushroom cloud. The explosion flattened everything in its path. More than 62,000 buildings were destroyed.

The first impact of the lightning flash and fireball was terrifying enough. Then came the powerful force of the shock waves, crushing buildings and hurling people through the air. The heat flash and the blast started fires all over the city, which were quickly fanned into a firestorm by the shock waves and winds. Many people who survived the first explosion died while trapped in their burning houses.

The city streets were filled with confusion and horror. People dug their way out of the rubble and tried to find some way to escape. But burned victims and dead bodies were everywhere. People were disoriented, since most landmarks had disappeared and the air was thick with dust.

Thousands of panicked victims jumped into the rivers that flowed through the city to try to escape the flames or soothe the burns covering their bodies. Many drowned, and soon the rivers were choked with corpses, which the current slowly carried toward the sea. One man tried to use the dead bodies as a bridge, crawling on his hands and knees over the corpses. He made it almost

Very few buildings remained standing after Hiroshima was bombed.

halfway across when a corpse sank beneath him and he had to crawl back to avoid being drowned.

Throughout that day and into the night, the survivors struggled to stay alive and bring help to the wounded and dying. Fires still raged, and two-thirds of the city's buildings had been ruined. On top of this, public utilities had been destroyed, cutting off water and electricity. Most hospitals were damaged, and 90 percent of doctors, nurses, and other medical staff had been killed or badly wounded.

Volunteers began to stack the bodies into piles, pour oil on them, and burn them. After a couple of days, however, the task was abandoned. There were too many bodies to be stacked, and the smell of decay hung in the air. This stench mingled with the smells of fires and dust to produce an odor some compared to burning sardines.

On August 6 in Washington, D.C., 16 hours after the attack on Hiroshima, President Truman issued a

A SURVIVOR'S STORY

Dr. Michihiko Hachiya, who survived the Hiroshima bombing, kept a diary of what happened on August 6, 1945, and the days that followed.

Hachiya lived about one mile (1.6 km) from the target site. After the explosion he was in the ruins of his house, naked and bleeding from several wounds. His wife, Yaeko-san, was also wounded, but less severely. They made their way outside, where buildings were swaying and collapsing. They tried to walk the few hundred yards to the Communications Hospital, where Hachiya was the director, but Hachiya collapsed. He told his wife to go ahead and get help, and then passed out from loss of blood. When he awoke, he thought at first he was surrounded by walking ghosts. These were people so badly burned that they were holding their arms out to stop the raw flesh from rubbing against their clothes.

When Hachiya finally reached the hospital, he found that part

74

statement. "The force from which the sun draws its power," he said, "has been loosed against those who brought war to the Far East . . . We spent two billion dollars on the greatest scientific gamble in history—and won."

of it was in flames, but workers there managed to put out the fire. He found his wife, who had been treated, and spent the night at the hospital. The morning after the bombing, he woke up to sunlight shining through gaping holes where windows had been blown out. All around him were moaning patients. There were so many wounded that they were placed in the bathrooms, beneath the stairway, and even in the garden in front of the hospital. Many had been near the city center when the bomb fell. The few staff members who were able to work struggled to feed and care for the 150 patients. "Everything was in disorder," he wrote in his diary. "And to make matters worse was the vomiting and diarrhea . . . persons entering or leaving the hospital could not avoid stepping in the filth, so closely was it spread."

Hachiya went back to work at the hospital as soon as he could. He kept his diary until September 30, 1945. Ten years later he published the diary as a book, *Hiroshima Diary: The Journal of a Japanese Physician, August 6–September 30, 1945.*

A cloud of smoke rose more than 60,000 feet (18,290 m) in the air after the second atomic bomb exploded over the city of Nagasaki.

CHAPTER EIGHT

SECOND INFERNO

News of the tragedy in Hiroshima didn't reach Tokyo, Japan's capital, for many hours. Not until August 8 did the Japanese government issue a statement condemning the United States and its actions. But the Japanese leaders still wouldn't surrender.

The Americans tried to reach out to Japanese citizens to ask them to persuade Japanese leaders to surrender. They dropped leaflets and broadcast messages that said, "We are in possession of the most destructive weapon ever designed by man. This is an awful fact for you to ponder. We have just begun to use this weapon against your homeland. If you still have any doubt, ask about what happened to Hiroshima when just one atomic bomb fell on that city. . . . We ask that you now petition your Emperor to end the war."

While the Japanese leaders argued about what to do, an operation to drop a second bomb on Japan was already underway. The target was Kokura, a coastal town on the island of Kyushu, southwest of Hiroshima. Kokura was one of Japan's biggest storage areas for weapons and ammunition.

Long before dawn on August 9, another heavily loaded B-29 took off from the U.S. Air Force base on Tinian. The plane was named *Bockscar*, after Frederick Bock, the pilot who usually flew it. But that day Major Chuck Sweeney piloted *Bockscar*. The bomb's nickname was "Fat Man," because it was much bigger than Little Boy. By midmorning, *Bockscar* was circling high above the north coast of Kyushu.

The weather saved Kokura. The town was covered with low clouds, as well as ground fog and smoke. After circling the town twice, Sweeney decided he couldn't see the target area clearly enough. His B-29 was low on fuel, and he couldn't afford to wait. So he turned and flew south toward the secondary target, Nagasaki.

The Nagasaki bomb crew flew a B-29 bomber they called *Bockscar*.

With a population of about 240,000, Nagasaki was one of Japan's oldest and biggest ports and home to a large number of Japanese Christians. It was also an important center of shipbuilding and other industries, including a weapons factory. On this fateful morning, the city was also covered in clouds. Sweeney considered giving up and dropping his very expensive cargo into the ocean on the way home.

But the clouds suddenly parted, and at about 11 a.m. *Bockscar* dropped Fat Man on the city. It exploded about 1,650 feet (500 m) above Nagasaki.

Fat Man detonated with an even greater force than Little Boy had, but it caused less damage to the city's buildings. Hiroshima was on very flat land, so the blast traveled straight outward from the center. The steep hills that surround Nagasaki absorbed some of the shock and stopped the blast from spreading. Even so, the blast immediately killed or fatally wounded about 45,000 people.

Only a few hundred people had taken refuge in underground bomb shelters. Anyone within about 3,000 feet (915 m) of the blast was burned to ash within seconds. Those farther away suffered scorched, blistering wounds. Many other people were hit by flying rubble or were trapped in collapsed buildings. Fires broke out, but there was no firestorm as there had been at Hiroshima.

That evening Japanese leaders met in an underground bunker in Tokyo to discuss their options. Even after the death and destruction, the military leaders didn't want to give up. They would rather die than endure the shame of surrender.

On August 9 Japan's Emperor Hirohito gave a speech to his war council. "I cannot bear to see my innocent people struggle any longer," he said. "Ending the war is the only way to restore world peace and to relieve the nation from the terrible distress with which it is burdened."

Even suburbs 4 miles (6.4 km) outside of the center of Nagaski where the atomic bomb was dropped suffered devastation.

The others accepted his advice, and next morning they agreed to surrender—with one condition. They refused to allow the Allies to take the emperor's power. At the time the Japanese viewed their emperors as living gods, and stripping the emperor of his power was unthinkable to them.

President Truman refused to agree to this condition. The emperor would have to be under the control of the Allied leaders. But the president secretly ordered the atomic bombing to stop. He said the thought of wiping out another 100,000 people was too horrible. Even so,

The formal surrender ceremony took place on the USS *Missouri* in Tokyo Bay on September 2, 1945.

B-29s went on bombing Japanese cities with ordinary high-explosive bombs.

The emperor called a meeting of his war council on August 14, 1945, and told them he wanted Japan to surrender. At midday on August 15, Hirohito announced the surrender in a four-minute radio address to the Japanese people. Few of them had ever heard his voice before.

Hirohito didn't use the word *surrender* in his speech. He placed the blame on the deployment of the atomic bomb. He informed the people that Japan's military would put down their arms in order to ensure world peace. "Should we continue to fight, not only would it result in an ultimate collapse and obliteration of the Japanese nation, but also it would lead to the total extinction of human civilization," he said.

When the news of the surrender reached the United States and Europe, people celebrated in the streets. World War II was finally over.

The Hiroshima Railroad Station was one of the first buildings to be rebuilt after the bombing.

CHAPTER NINE

THE AFTERMATH

A couple of weeks after the bombings, most survivors in Hiroshima and Nagasaki thought the worst was over. Many were recovering from their wounds. But then some survivors started to have strange symptoms. Many developed patches of tiny purple spots under their skin. On some people the number of spots began to increase. Their hair fell out and they grew weaker and thinner every day. They suffered from diarrhea and vomiting. They had radiation sickness—the result of the deadly rays released by the fission of the uranium and plutonium atoms in the bombs.

Slowly the death rates began to rise again. People who had been near the center of the blast and escaped injury developed radiation sickness, and so did many who had been much farther away. Some died within two days, and nearly all died within a week. Doctors in Hiroshima and Nagasaki gradually realized that they were seeing a completely new kind of disease, which at first they called "atomic bomb illness."

The radiation had other harmful effects. Pregnant women who were within 3,000 feet (914 m) of the blast had miscarriages. Many of those farther away had babies who died soon after birth. Many men became sterile and could not father children for several months after the explosion.

For those who survived the blast and the radiation sickness, daily life was a struggle. Their communities had been destroyed. Hospitals, schools, police stations, restaurants, shops, theaters, temples, and offices no longer existed. Many people felt lost and helpless. An author in Hiroshima, Yoko Ota, wrote, "We were being killed against our will by something completely unknown to us. . . . It is the misery of being thrown into a world of new terror and fear, a world more unknown than that of people sick with cancer."

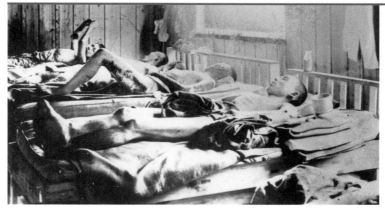

Many survivors of the bombing still suffered from the effects of radiation.

But life quickly began to return to the flattened streets of Hiroshima and Nagasaki. Thousands of people escaped to the hills immediately after the bombs had exploded. Now they returned, searching for the places where their homes had once stood. Hiroshima's newspaper began publishing again on August 31, 1945. Electricity was restored in several areas on September 10.

Help from other countries and organizations also began to arrive. The Allies didn't want to repeat the mistake they had made after World War I in punishing the defeated countries. Allied troops, under the command of U.S. Army General Douglas MacArthur, established bases in Japan and began helping the country rebuild. Along with changing Japan's constitution, the

Allies established land reform laws that increased the rights of Japan's small farmers, gave more rights to women, and encouraged an economy based on industry rather than agriculture.

The Japanese government also did whatever it could to help its people. The government distributed emergency food rations and set up makeshift hospitals. Soldiers were sent from Tokyo to clear dead bodies and the worst of the rubble. Also, 24 new government offices were opened to sell food. The Hiroshima city government announced that it would give free building materials to anyone who asked.

In January 1946, a new government department began work in Hiroshima. Its job was to plan the rebuilding of the city in a modern way, with wide, straight avenues instead of narrow, winding streets and open parks instead of tiny gardens. But first the department had to decide whether the new city should be built on the scorched, radioactive soil where the old city had stood. A few weeks later, as spring arrived, something amazing happened that gave them an answer.

Near the Town Hall were two cherry trees. They appeared blackened and dead, ready to be cut down for firewood like all the other trees in the city. Then, one morning in April, they began to blossom with the white flowers that the Japanese especially cherish.

By the summer of 1946, large parts of the city were alive again. Hungry people planted any available land with crops. Potatoes, tomatoes, cabbages, and even rice were grown where the town center had once been. American troops gave out bags of cornmeal. But most Japanese people had never seen cornmeal before. Even with U.S. aid, thousands went hungry.

Rebuilding efforts in Hiroshima and Nagasaki were going very slowly. There was not enough money to pay for the materials and labor. In 1948 Hiroshima's mayor, Shinzo Hamai, started a campaign called "Help Hiroshima." He went to the Japanese parliament in Tokyo and begged for more money to get the city back on its feet.

Parliament passed a law on May 11, 1949, declaring that Hiroshima was to be called "The City of Peace." Hiroshima would have a special importance in Japan and would be given a lot of money to help with rebuilding. Not surprisingly, this angered the people of Nagasaki. Parliament quickly passed another law giving Nagasaki the title of "City of International Culture" and a smaller grant of money.

Now major work could begin. Armies of workers moved into the centers of both cities, demolishing wooden shacks, clearing away rubble, and digging foundations for new streets and apartments. One of the first buildings completed in Hiroshima was a new baseball stadium.

The Allied occupation of Japan lasted until 1952, although the country remained under U.S. military protection. Japan's economy began one of the fastest periods of growth in world history. The economy grew 9 percent each year between 1955 and 1973. Much of the growth came from manufacturing plants. Electronics companies such as Sony and Toshiba, auto manufacturers such as Honda and Toyota, and motorcycle companies such as Kawasaki and Yamaha made products that were sold all over the world, grabbing a huge share of the market. By 1968 Japan's economy was ranked second only to that of the United States.

A THOUSAND PAPER CRANES

Survivors who did not develop radiation sickness had another worry. The radiation caused some of the survivors to develop cancer. Some cancers showed up quickly, but others appeared years later.

Sadako Sasaki was only 2 years old when she survived the Hiroshima blast. When she was 11, she was diagnosed with leukemia, a type of blood cancer. As she lay in a hospital, she started folding origami paper birds called cranes, which are a Japanese symbol of long life and good luck. According to Japanese legend, if a sick person folds 1,000 cranes, the gods will heal him or her. Sadako decided to fold 1,000 cranes.

During the next 14 months, Sadako's friends and family saved paper scraps and candy wrappers for her. She folded them until she died October 25, 1955. She was 12 years old. Her death prompted a movement to build a monument to honor her and other children who died. A statue of her holding a crane was erected in Hiroshima's Peace Park. Every day visitors bring paper cranes to place next to the statue.

The United States detonated "Mike," the world's first hydrogen bomb, on November 1, 1952.

CHAPTER TEN

THE COLD WAR

The Japanese people had another cause for worry in October 1949. Soviet leaders announced that they had built and tested an atomic bomb. Now the United States and the Soviet Union—the two strongest countries in the world—both had nuclear weapons. The Soviet Union was determined to spread communism to other countries, especially in Eastern Europe. China, also a communist country, wanted communism to spread through Asia. The capitalist countries of the West, including Great Britain and the United States, wanted to stop the spread of communism. This conflict flared up in Korea. Communist troops from North Korea invaded South Korea, a U.S. ally, in June 1950. The invasion sparked the Korean War.

Even though the Korean War endangered the world, it was good for Hiroshima. The soldiers fighting communists in Korea came from many countries, all of which belonged to the United Nations. Hiroshima was the perfect place for U.N. forces to buy their equipment

The Korean War lasted three years and was the first military conflict of the Cold War.

and supplies. Before World War II, it had been a major center for weapons factories, and the old plants were rebuilt to meet the new demand for weapons. Over the next three years, Hiroshima prospered. New houses, office blocks, streets, parks, railways, shops, and restaurants sprang up across the city.

The war in Korea clearly showed that the world had divided into two camps after World War II. The communist Soviet Union and the democratic United States each led a group of nations. Each side distrusted the other and struggled to increase its power and influence. The struggle rarely led to actual battles, so the conflict was known as the Cold War.

The risk of using atomic bombs likely prevented another world war. But the two sides engaged in an arms race. The United States in 1952 produced the hydrogen bomb, which produced a much more powerful explosion than the atomic bomb. Less than a year later, the Soviet Union began making its own hydrogen bombs. By 1960 both sides were able to fire long-distance missiles armed with nuclear warheads.

The Americans and the Soviets both built huge stockpiles of the nuclear weapons. Soon there were enough nuclear bombs to destroy Earth several times over. Each nation threatened to use them if the other side used theirs first. This situation was called MAD, for mutual assured destruction.

The threat of nuclear war loomed over the world for 45 years after World War II. Both sides had equipment that could send deadly missiles across the world. The smallest error might have caused nuclear warfare that made the entire surface of Earth look like Hiroshima and Nagasaki.

The Cold War ended in 1991 with the collapse of the Soviet Union, but the nuclear threat remains. Today many countries are able to build nuclear weapons, and there is a growing concern that terrorist groups will be able to gain control of nuclear weapons.

Hiroshima and Nagasaki are still the only cities to have experienced a nuclear attack. Though they are now thriving cities, the Japanese have never forgotten their place in history. Today both are centers for international peace campaigns, and people come from all over the world to visit their museums and monuments.

Every anniversary of the bombings of Hiroshima and Nagasaki is a reminder of how quickly all life on Earth could be wiped away. Remembering how hundreds of thousands of people lost their lives encourages the nations of the world to work together to make sure it never happens.

REMEMBERING THE TRAGEDY

August 6, 1946, was the first anniversary of what the Japanese called the *pikadon*—a word referring to the "flash-boom" of the atomic bomb's explosion. The people of Hiroshima placed thousands of white lanterns in the Ota River, which carried them away to the sea. Each lantern was marked with the name of someone who had been killed or was missing.

The anniversary celebration in 1947 was much bigger. It was called the Festival of Peace and lasted for three days. The streets were filled with the noise of singing, dancing, processions, and fireworks.

In the years after the war, the two cities built memorials to the dead. In Hiroshima, a Garden of Peace was built on an island in the Ohta River, linked to the mainland by a Bridge of Peace. At one end of the garden stands the Atomic Bomb Dome, the remains of one of the few buildings not destroyed by the blast. At the other end is the Memorial Monument for Hiroshima. It is an arch shape in the style of old Japanese houses, with the simple inscription "Let all the souls here rest in peace, for we shall not repeat the evil."

A stone chest in the monument holds the names of those killed by the bomb. About 80,000 died on August 6, 1945, but the total number of people killed has never stopped rising. The deadly curse of radiation continues to find victims. As of August 6, 2016, more than 300,000 names were listed in 110 volumes in the chest, and there was one volume for the unidentified.

In Nagasaki, a Peace Park was built. A giant statue of a seated man is in the park, its right hand pointing upward. It is a permanent warning to be on guard against destruction from the sky. Its horizontal left hand symbolizes peace.

TIMELINE

▶ **1915**
Albert Einstein publishes his general theory of relativity

▶ **1931**
Japan invades Manchuria in China

▶ **1933**
Adolf Hitler becomes chancellor of Germany; laws persecuting Jews are passed in Germany; Einstein and other German scientists leave the country

▶ **1938**
Otto Hahn, Lise Meitner, and Fritz Strassmann split an atom of uranium into two pieces

▶ **September 1, 1939**
Germany invades Poland, beginning World War II

▶ **April 1941**
Japanese army leaders approve research about atomic weapons

▶ **December 7, 1941**
Japanese attack U.S. Pacific Fleet in Pearl Harbor, Hawaii

▶ **September 1942**
Atomic bomb project
is code-named the
Manhattan Project

▶ **December 2, 1942**
Italian physicist
Enrico Fermi oversees
construction of an
atomic pile at the
University of Chicago;
it is used to create the
first sustainable nuclear
chain reaction

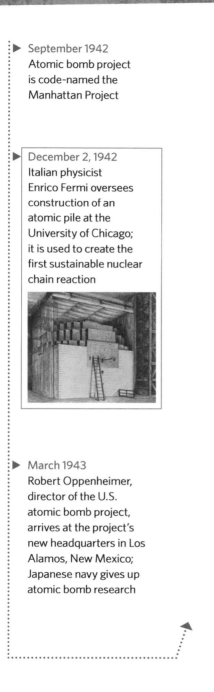

▶ **March 1943**
Robert Oppenheimer,
director of the U.S.
atomic bomb project,
arrives at the project's
new headquarters in Los
Alamos, New Mexico;
Japanese navy gives up
atomic bomb research

▶ **June 1944**
Army Air Corps Colonel
Paul Tibbets is given
command of the 509th
Composite Group on
Tinian for the atomic
bomb mission

▶ **March 10, 1945**
U.S. B-29s make
bombing raid on Tokyo,
killing 100,000 people

▶ **April 12, 1945**
President Roosevelt
dies; Harry S. Truman
becomes president

▶ **May 8, 1945**
Germany surrenders to
Allied forces; war ends
in Europe

► July 16, 1945
Trinity test explodes
atomic bomb
at Alamogordo,
New Mexico

► July 26, 1945
Allies broadcast demand
for Japanese surrender;
Japanese refuse

► August 6, 1945
First atomic bomb,
Little Boy, dropped on
Hiroshima from B-29
Enola Gay; about
80,000 people die
within seconds

► August 9, 1945
Second atomic bomb,
Fat Man, dropped on
Nagasaki; about 45,000
people are killed or
mortally injured

► August 15, 1945
Japan surrenders
unconditionally, ending
World War II

► August 1946
First anniversary of the
Hiroshima bombing is
quietly commemorated

► August 1947
Three-day Festival of
Peace commemorates
second anniversary of
Hiroshima bombing

▶ May 1949
Japanese Parliament declares Hiroshima "City of Peace" and Nagasaki "City of International Culture"

▶ October 1949
Soviet Union announces successful test of atomic bomb

▶ June 1950
Korean War begins

▶ August 1952
Memorial tower for victims of Hiroshima and Nagasaki unveiled

▶ November 1952
United States explodes first hydrogen bomb, which is 700 times as powerful as Little Boy

▶ July 1953
Korean War ends

GLOSSARY

aircraft carrier—ship that carries warplanes and helicopters and has a flight deck for takeoffs and landings

bomb bay—chamber in the belly of a bomber that holds bombs during flight

capitalism—economic system in which goods and the ways of making them are owned by individuals or companies

chain reaction—self-sustaining chemical or nuclear reaction yielding energy or products that cause further reactions of the same kind

communism—system in which goods and property are owned by the government and shared in common; communist rulers limit personal freedoms to achieve their goals

detonate—to set off an explosion

electron—particle that orbits the nucleus of an atom and has a negative electrical charge

fission—splitting of an atomic nucleus resulting in the release of large amounts of energy

isotope—one of various forms of an element that have differing numbers of neutrons

leukemia—form of cancer that affects blood cells

neutron—particle in the nucleus of an atom; neutrons have no electrical charge

nuclear—type of energy created by splitting atoms; nuclear bombs use the energy to cause an explosion

nucleus—central part of an atom, made up of neutrons and protons

particle—basic unit of matter and energy, such as an atom or molecule

physicist—scientist who studies matter and energy and how they interact

plutonium—radioactive metallic element

proton—particle in the nucleus of an atom that has a positive electrical charge

radiation—emission of energy in the form of waves or particles from a substance that has unstable atomic nuclei

shock wave—burst of quickly moving air, such as waves caused by an explosion

uranium— radioactive silvery-white element

FURTHER READING

Marcovitz, Hal. *The Making of the Atomic Bomb.*
San Diego: ReferencePoint Press, 2015.

Peppas, Lynn. *Hiroshima and Nagasaki.*
St. Catharines, Ontario: Crabtree Publishing, 2013.

Stelson, Caren. *Sachiko: A Nagasaki Bomb Survivor's Story.*
Minneapolis: Carolrhoda Books, 2016.

Wukovits, John F. *The Manhattan Project.*
Farmington Hills, Mich.: Lucent Books, 2014.

INTERNET SITES

Use FactHound to find Internet sites related to this book.

Visit *www.facthound.com*
Just type in 9780756555849 and go.

CRITICAL THINKING QUESTIONS

President Harry Truman said he decided to drop the two atomic bombs in order to end the war and save many more lives than would have been lost if the war had continued. Do you agree with his decision? Why or why not?

If nuclear weapons had never been invented, do you think the world would still be fighting major wars as in the past? Support your answer with evidence from the text.

What was it like to grow up in Japan after the nuclear bombings? How were Japanese children's lives different from those in other parts of the world, such as the United States? Support your answer with evidence from the text.

SOURCE NOTES

Page 8, line 3: Arata Osada. *Children of the A-bomb, the Testament of the Boys and Girls of Hiroshima*. Trans. Jean Dan and Ruth Sieben-Morgan. New York: Putnam, 1963, p. 157.

Page 8, line 11: Ibid.

Page 8, line 19: Ibid., pp. 157–158.

Page 20, line 11: Richard Rhodes. *The Making of the Atomic Bomb*. New York: Simon & Schuster, 1986, p. 713.

Page 36, line 8: "Einstein-Szilard Letter." 2 Aug. 1939. 8 Feb. 2017. Atomic Heritage Foundation. http://www.atomicheritage.org/key-documents/einstein-szilard-letter

Page 38, line 12: "The Einstein Letter—1939." 8 Feb. 2017. Atomic Heritage Foundation. http://www.atomicheritage.org/history/einstein-letter-1939

Page 38, line 14: Ibid.

Page 38, line 16: Ibid.

Page 47, line 3: *The Making of the Atomic Bomb*, p. 406.

Page 48, line 16: "The Manhattan Project: Making the Atomic Bomb." 8 Feb. 2017. Atomic Archive. http://www.atomicarchive.com/History/mp/p2s15.shtml

Page 50, col. 2, line 4: "The Unlikely Pair." 8 Feb. 2017. Atomic Heritage Foundation. http://www.atomicheritage.org/history/unlikely-pair

Page 51, line 17: Spencer R. Weart and Gertrud Weiss Szilard, eds. *Leo Szilard, His Version of the Facts: Selected Recollections and Correspondence*. Cambridge, Mass.: MIT Press, 1978, p. 146.

Page 53, col. 1, line 4: *The Making of the Atomic Bomb*, p. 440.

Page 60, line 7: I.I. Rabi. *Science: The Center of Culture*. New York: World Pub. Co., 1970, p. 138.

Page 61, line 9: Robert Jungk. *Brighter than a Thousand Suns: A Personal History of the Atomic Scientists*. Trans. James Cleugh. New York: Harcourt Brace, 1958, p. 183.

Page 65, line 5: *The Making of the Atomic Bomb*, p. 700.

Page 71, line 13: Ibid., p. 711.

Page 75, line 1: "Press Release by the White House, August 6, 1945." 8 Feb. 2017. Harry S. Truman Library & Museum. https://www.trumanlibrary. org/whistlestop/study_collections/bomb/large/documents/index. php?documentdate=1945-08-06&documentid=59&pagenumber=1

Page 75, col. 2, line 2: Michihiko Hachiya, M.D. *Hiroshima Diary: The Journal of a Japanese Physician, August 6–September 30, 1945: Fifty Years Later.* Trans. and ed. Warner Wells, M.D. Chapel Hill: University of North Carolina Press, 1995, pp. 11–12.

Page 77, line 9: Adrian Weale, ed. *Eyewitness Hiroshima: First-Hand Accounts of the Atomic Terror That Changed the World.* London: Carroll & Graf Publishers, 1995, p. 244.

Page 81, line 2: Ibid., p. 259.

Page 83, line 13: Max Fisher. "The Emperor's Speech: 67 Years Ago, Hirohito Transformed Japan Forever." *The Atlantic.* 15 Aug. 2012. 8 Feb. 2017. https:// www.theatlantic.com/international/archive/2012/08/the-emperors-speech-67-years-ago-hirohito-transformed-japan-forever/261166

Page 86, line 17: *The Making of the Atomic Bomb,* p. 732.

Page 98, col. 2, line 14: Cenotaph for the A-bomb Victims (Memorial Monument for Hiroshima, City of Peace). Hiroshima Navigator. 8 Feb. 2017. http://www. hiroshima-navi.or.jp/en/sightseeing/hibaku_ireihi/ireihi/21535.php

SELECT BIBLIOGRAPHY

Atomic Archive. 8 Feb. 2017. http://www.atomicarchive.com

Atomic Heritage Foundation. 8 Feb. 2017. http://www.atomicheritage.org

Cenotaph for the A-bomb Victims (Memorial Monument for Hiroshima, City of Peace). Hiroshima Navigator. 8 Feb. 2017. http://www.hiroshima-navi.or.jp/en/sightseeing/hibaku_ireihi/ireihi/21535.php

Fisher, Max. "The Emperor's Speech: 67 Years Ago, Hirohito Transformed Japan Forever." *The Atlantic.* 15 Aug. 2012. 8 Feb. 2017. https://www.theatlantic.com/international/archive/2012/08/the-emperors-speech-67-years-ago-hirohito-transformed-japan-forever/261166

Groves, Leslie R. *Now It Can Be Told: The Story of the Manhattan Project.* New York: Harper, 1962.

Hachiya, Michihiko, M.D. *Hiroshima Diary: The Journal of a Japanese Physician, August 6–September 30, 1945: Fifty Years Later.* Trans. and ed. Warner Wells, M.D. Chapel Hill: University of North Carolina Press, 1995.

Ham, Paul. *Hiroshima, Nagasaki: The Real Story of the Atomic Bombings and Their Aftermath.* New York: Thomas Dunne Books, St. Martin's Press, 2014.

Hiroshima Peace Memorial Museum. 8 Feb. 2017. http://www.pcf.city.hiroshima.jp/index_e2.html

Jungk, Robert. *Brighter than a Thousand Suns: A Personal History of the Atomic Scientists.* Trans. James Cleugh. New York: Harcourt Brace, 1958.

Jungk, Robert. *Children of the Ashes: The Story of a Rebirth.* Trans. Constantine Fitzgibbon. New York: Harcourt Brace, 1961.

"The Manhattan Project." American Museum of Natural History. 8 Feb. 2017. http://www.amnh.org/exhibitions/einstein/peace-and-war/the-manhattan-project

Osada, Arata. *Children of the A-bomb, the Testament of the Boys and Girls of Hiroshima.* Trans. Jean Dan and Ruth Sieben-Morgan. New York: Putnam, 1963.

"Primary Sources: Announcing the Bombing of Hiroshima." *American Experience.* PBS. 8 Feb. 2017. http://www.pbs.org/wgbh/americanexperience/features/primary-resources/truman-hiroshima

Rabi, I.I. *Science: The Center of Culture.* New York: World Pub. Co., 1970.

Rhodes, Richard. *The Making of the Atomic Bomb.* New York: Simon & Schuster, 1986.

Thomas, Gordon, and Max Morgan Witts. *Ruin from the Air: The Enola Gay's Atomic Mission to Hiroshima.* Chelsea, Mich.: Scarborough House, 1990.

Weale, Adrian, ed. *Eyewitness Hiroshima: First-Hand Accounts of the Atomic Terror That Changed the World.* London: Carroll & Graf Publishers, 1995.

Weart, Spencer R., and Gertrud Weiss Szilard, eds. *Leo Szilard, His Version of the Facts: Selected Recollections and Correspondence.* Cambridge, Mass.: MIT Press, 1978.

INDEX